KU-646-638

The Driving Standards Agency (DSA) is an Executive Agency of the Department of Transport. You will see its logo at test centres.

DRIVING
STANDARDS
AGENCY

"Safe driving for life"

The aim of DSA is to promote road safety through the advancement of driving standards.

DSA

- Conducts practical driving tests for drivers or riders of cars, motorcycles, lorries, buses and other vehicles

- Plans, maintains and supervises the theory test for drivers or riders of cars, motorcycles, lorries and buses

- Controls the register of Approved Driving Instructors (ADIs)

- Supervises Compulsory Basic Training (CBT) for motorcyclists

- Aims to provide a high-quality service to its customers

Each year nearly 1 million people decide they want to learn to drive a car or to ride a moped or motorcycle. You and most of the others will go on to take the driving tests.

The purpose of the tests is to prove that you can drive your vehicle safely on the road. Therefore, it's vitally important to develop the correct attitude towards driving, showing responsibility and consideration to other road users. Only those who can do this will earn the right to drive without L plates (or D plates in Wales), and on motorways.

By passing your tests you will have proved that you have learned the theory, but it's important that you understand the principles of what you have learned and put them into practice. The instruction you receive before the tests is the foundation for gaining further skills and experience. The tests are just one stage in your driving or riding career. You shouldn't assume that if you pass your tests you are a good driver or rider with nothing more to learn.

During your practical test your examiner will want to see you driving to the standards set in this book. Those standards are given here in an easy-to-read style with illustrations, which explain simply what is required. However, driving is never predictable. Road conditions or circumstances will demand that you use your initiative or common sense. You should be able to assess any situation and apply the guidance given in this book to it.

Make sure that your aim is '*Safe driving for life*'.

Robin Cummins
Chief Driving Examiner
Driving Standards Agency

This book will help you to

▶ **Learn to drive competently**

▶ **Prepare and help you to pass your practical driving test**

Part One tells you what you need to do before the test.

Part Two gives the test requirements with simple, clear advice. Refer to it regularly and use it to check your progress.

Part Three shows what is required if you need to take a test to tow a trailer.

Part Four will tell you all you need to know if you are a learner moped rider or a motorcyclist. There are full details about Compulsory Basic Training (CBT) and the motorcycle test.

Part Five gives details about the extended test for disqualified drivers and riders.

Part Six contains the official syllabus for learning to drive and lists the skills you need to learn before taking your test. Refer to it regularly.

The important factors

This book is only **one** of the important factors in your training. The others are

▶ **A good instructor**

▶ **Plenty of practice**

▶ **Your attitude**

You must manage your own learning.

Aim to be a safe and confident driver or rider for life, and not just to pass your test.

Driving is a life skill.

Your tests are just the beginning.

Books for study

It's strongly recommended that you study a copy of *The Highway Code*. You can order a copy when you apply for your licence or buy one from a good bookshop.

The DSA Driving Skills series of books will provide you with sound knowledge of driving and riding skills.

The Official Theory Test for Car Drivers and Motorcyclists, The Driving Manual and *The Motorcycling Manual* are all published by The Stationery Office.

A CD-ROM, *The Theory Test and Beyond* (The Stationery Office), provides a fun and modern way of learning.

PART ONE — BEFORE YOUR TEST

This part looks at how to prepare yourself for the test.

The topics covered

- The theory test
- About the driving test
- Preparing for your driving test
- When you are ready for your test
- How to apply for your test
- Before attending your driving test

Before you take your practical driving test you will have to take a theory test. If you pass that you will be given a pass certificate. You must take this with you when you attend your practical test.

DriveSafe Services Ltd conducts theory tests on behalf of DSA. There are over 150 theory test centres in Great Britain and Northern Ireland. Theory test sessions are available during weekdays, evenings and on Saturdays. If you wish to book a test, an appointment will be available for you within about two weeks (a bit longer if you have special needs).

You can find out where your local centre is from

- Your Approved Driving Instructor (ADI)
- A DSA driving test centre
- The telephone information line 0645 000 555

Study your copy of *The Highway Code* and the publication *The Official Theory Test for Car Drivers and Motorcyclists* (both published by The Stationery Office).

If you are well prepared you won't find the questions difficult. *The Official Theory Test for Car Drivers and Motorcyclists* will provide you with the questions and answers.

It's very important that you know why the answers are correct. Take this knowledge and put it into practice on the road. Your examiner will expect you to demonstrate what you have learned through your driving.

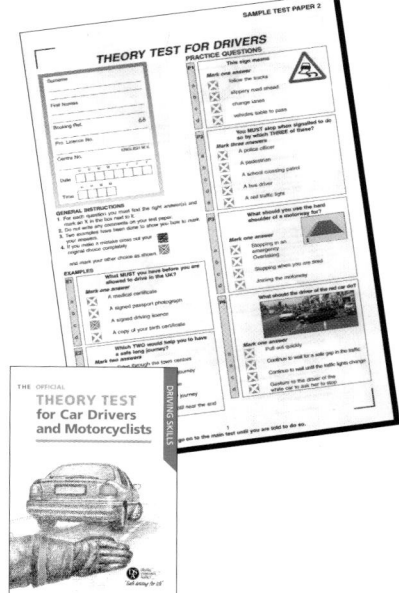

The driving test is straightforward

You will pass if you can show your examiner that you can

- Drive safely
- Complete the set exercises
- Demonstrate, through your driving, that you have a thorough knowledge of *The Highway Code*

Does the standard of the test vary?

No. All examiners are trained to carry out the test to the same standard.

Test routes

- Are as uniform as possible
- Include a range of typical road and traffic conditions

You should have the same result from different examiners or at different test centres.

Are the examiners supervised?

Yes, they are closely supervised. A senior officer may sit in on your test.

Don't worry about this. The senior officer won't be examining you, but making sure the examiner is testing you properly. The senior officer won't interfere with the test, so just carry on as if he or she wasn't there.

Can anyone accompany me on the test?

Yes, your instructor is allowed to be present during the test but must not take any part in it.

You should bring an interpreter with you if you need one, but you must not use an Approved Driving Instructor (ADI) for that purpose. Your interpreter must be 16 years or over and wear suitable seat restraints where they are available.

Can I use a car which is 'automatic' for the test?

Yes. When you pass your practical test your full driving licence will entitle you to drive an 'automatic' car. It will also act as a provisional licence for a car with a manual gearbox.

Your provisional driving licence

You must hold a valid, signed provisional driving licence before you attempt to drive on the road.

Ask for the application form D1 at a post office.

When you receive your licence, sign it. It isn't valid until you have done so.

Using an Approved Driving Instructor (ADI)

An Approved Driving Instructor is approved by DSA to teach learner drivers for payment.

DSA is responsible for maintaining and checking the standards of all ADIs.

ADIs must

- Have held a full driving licence for at least four years
- Pass a written exam lasting 90 minutes
- Pass a strict driving test
- Reach and keep up a high standard of instruction. ADIs are regularly checked by a supervising examiner from DSA
- Be registered with DSA
- Display an ADI identification certificate on the windscreen of the tuition vehicle

You must use an ADI or a trainee licence-holder if you want to learn the practical skills of driving and pay someone to teach you.

It is unlikely that anyone except an ADI would have the experience, knowledge and training to teach you properly.

Some trainee driving instructors are granted a trainee licence so that they can gain teaching experience before their qualifying examination. This licence is a pink identification certificate which must be displayed on the windscreen of the tuition vehicle.

Take advice from your ADI on

- All aspects of driving
- What books to read
- When you will be ready for your test
- How to practise

How to choose an ADI

- Ask friends and relatives
- Choose an instructor
  - who has a good reputation
  - is reliable and punctual
  - whose car suits you

When you practise

If you are taking lessons with an ADI it's a good idea to take extra practice with a friend or relative. Ask your ADI for advice on this.

You must have with you a person who

- Has held a full driving licence for at least three years and still holds one for the category of vehicle being driven
- Is at least 21 years of age

Vehicle insurance

The vehicle you practise in must be properly insured for you to drive. You will be asked to sign a declaration before the test begins.

If you drive while uninsured you will be committing a serious offense.

Don't risk it.

Study *The Highway Code*

- Know and understand *The Highway Code*
- Obey it when driving

How and where to practise

Practise

- On as many different types of road as you can
- In all sorts of traffic conditions – even in the dark
- On dual carriageways where the upper speed limit applies

You may be asked to drive on such roads during the test. Don't just concentrate on exercises included in the test.

When you practise try not to

- Obstruct other traffic. Most drivers are tolerant of learners, but don't try their patience too much
- Annoy local residents. For example, by repeatedly practising emergency stops in quiet residential streets or by practising on test routes

When will I be ready for the test?

When you show that you have reached the standards set in this book – not before.

You should ensure that all of the aspects of the official syllabus have been covered (see Part Six).

The learners who pass first time do so because they are well instructed and get plenty of practice.

They pass because **they wait until they are ready.**

How will I know when I'm ready?

Your instructor has the knowledge and experience to tell you when you are ready.

You must be able to drive

- Consistently well and with confidence
- Without assistance and guidance from your instructor

If you can't, you aren't ready for the test. Waiting until you are ready will save you time and money.

Disabilities or special circumstances

To make sure that enough time is allowed for your test, it would help DSA to know if you

- Are deaf or have severe hearing difficulties
- Are in any way restricted in your movements
- Have any disability which may affect your driving

If any of these apply to you, please write this on your application form.

If you can't speak English or are deaf, you are allowed to bring an interpreter (who must not be an instructor). The interpreter must be 16 years or over.

No matter how serious your disability might be, you will still take the same driving test as every other test candidate. However, more time is allowed for the test. This is simply so that your examiner can talk to you about your disability and any adaptations fitted to your vehicle.

If you would like further information, please see the list of useful addresses at the back of this book.

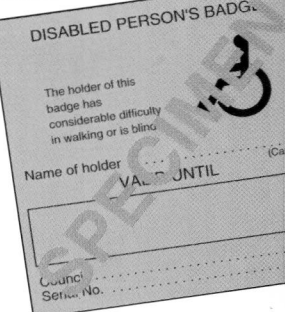

DISABLED PERSON'S BADGE

The holder of this badge has considerable difficulty in walking or is blind

Name of holder ....

VALID UNTIL

Council ....
Serial No. ....

SPECIMEN

The test application form

You can obtain an application form (DL26) at any DSA driving test centre. Your ADI will also be able to give you a copy and tell you the fee to send with it.

Full details of all fees can be obtained from DSA Area Offices or from your nearest driving test centre.

Complete the form and send it to your DSA Area Office. You will find the address on the back of the form.

At test centres in Wales, you may wish to take a test in the Welsh language. Please indicate your choice on the test application form.

- Apply well before the time you want to be tested
- Give your preferred date

Booking by credit or debit card

You must be the card-holder. If you aren't, then the card-holder must be present when a booking is made on the telephone. Visa, Mastercard, Switch and Delta are all accepted.

The credit card telephone number for your area is shown on the application form and in the list of DSA Area Offices at the back of this book.

If you use this service the driving test booking clerk will be able to offer you an appointment over the telephone. You should receive written notification confirming the appointment within a few days.

When you telephone, make sure that you have the completed application form with you.

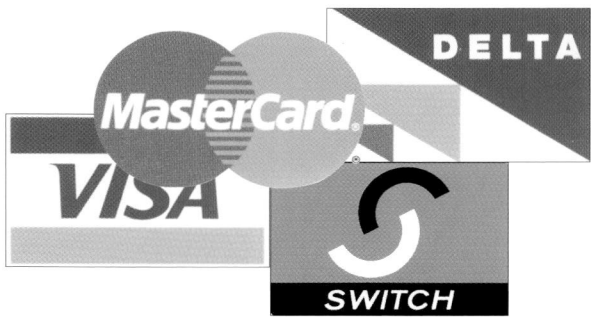

DSA THE DRIVING TEST

The booking clerk will want to know the following details

- Your driver number shown on your licence
- The type of test you wish to book
- Your personal details (name, address, day/evening telephone numbers)
- Driving school code number (if known)
- Your preferred date
- Unacceptable days or periods
- If you can accept a test at short notice (consult your ADI beforehand, if necessary)
- Disability or any special circumstances
- Your credit card number and its expiry date and issue number, when using Switch

Saturday and evening tests

Saturday and weekday evening tests are available at some driving test centres. The fees for these are higher than for a driving test during the normal working hours on weekdays. Evening tests are available during the summer months only.

You can get details from

- DSA Area Offices
- Driving test centres
- Your ADI

Driving test fees

You may pay by

- Cheque
- Postal order
- Credit card

Don't send cash.

Your test appointment

Your DSA Area Office will send you notification of your appointment, which is the receipt of your fee. Take this with you when you go for your test.

This will include

- The time and place of your test
- The address of the driving test centre
- Other important information

If you haven't received notification after two weeks, contact the Area Office.

Postponing your test appointment

Contact the DSA Area Office where you booked your test if

- The date or time of the appointment isn't suitable
- You want to postpone or cancel your test

You must give at least ten clear **working days'** notice (that is, two weeks – longer if there is a bank holiday) not counting

- The day the Area Office received your request
- The day of the test

If you don't give enough notice you will lose your fee.

DSA THE DRIVING TEST

Documents

Make sure that you have your provisional driving licence **and** your theory test pass certificate with you when you arrive for your test. Check that you have signed your licence. Any of the following licences are acceptable

- A provisional driving licence issued in Great Britain (GB), or a GB full licence giving the provisional entitlement
- A provisional licence issued in Northern Ireland (NI), or a full licence giving the provisional entitlement
- An EU licence accompanied by a GB provisional licence, if you want to take a test for a category not covered by your full EU licence

If you have a full category B licence (cars) which was issued in another country but isn't eligible for exchange for a GB licence, you must apply for, and bring with you, a GB provisional licence. For information see DVLA information sheet D100, which is available from post offices.

Your examiner might not be able to conduct the test if you can't produce one of these licences.

Photo identity

You will need to take with you a form of photographic identification. For this your examiner will accept

- A current signed passport. This doesn't have to be a British passport
- Any of the following identification cards, provided it has your photograph and your signature
  - workplace identity card
  - trade union or students' union membership card
  - card for the purchase of rail tickets
  - school bus pass
  - cheque guarantee card or credit card
- A photograph of yourself, which has been signed and dated on the back by an acceptable person, confirming that the photograph is a true likeness of you. A signature will be accepted from the following
  - Approved Driving Instructor
  - DSA certified motorcycle instructor
  - Member of Parliament
  - local authority councillor
  - teacher (qualified)
  - Justice of the Peace
  - civil servant (established)
  - police officer
  - bank official

- minister of religion
- barrister or solicitor
- medical practitioner

Your test will be cancelled if you can't provide one of these forms of identification.

Your test vehicle

Make sure that the vehicle you intend to drive or the motorcycle you intend to ride during the test is

- Legally roadworthy and has a current test certificate, if it's over the prescribed age
- Fully covered by insurance for its present use and for you to drive

Your examiner will ask you to sign a declaration that your insurance is in order. The test won't be conducted if you are unable to do so.

Note: A hire car is unlikely to be insured for the driving test. You should check with the hire company before you sign the declaration at the test centre.

Your vehicle should also display

- A valid tax disc (unless exempt)
- L plates or, if you wish, D plates, if taking your test in Wales, displayed to the front and rear

The plates shouldn't be displayed on the windscreen or back window. Both you and your examiner should have a clear view of the road.

If you overlook any of these

- Your test may be cancelled
- You could lose your fee

For details of the moped and motorcycle test see Part Four.

The condition of your vehicle

Your vehicle must be mechanically sound. All equipment required by law must be fitted and working correctly.

Many modern vehicles are equipped with a spare wheel intended for temporary use. Your vehicle won't be suitable to use for the test if one of these spare wheels is in use.

The controls, seating, equipment or any other articles in the vehicle must be arranged so that they don't interfere with the conduct of the test.

A dual accelerator (if fitted) must be removed before the test.

Your examiner must be able to see clearly through the rear windows.

Seat belts

If the law requires your vehicle to have seat belts, make sure that they

- Work properly
- Are clean and in a satisfactory condition

Wear your seat belt, unless you have a medical exemption certificate.

You are allowed to remove your seat belt to carry out a manoeuvre which involves reversing. Make sure that you refasten it immediately afterwards.

If your examiner isn't able to fasten a seat belt your test will be cancelled and you will lose your fee.

Head restraints

Most modern vehicles are fitted with head restraints to provide protection in the event of an accident or heavy braking. If your vehicle has them fitted please don't remove them before coming for your test.

Left-hand drive vehicles

If you are driving a left-hand drive vehicle, take special care and make full use of your mirrors.

Unsuitable vehicles for a car driving test

- Vehicles with no clear view to the rear – other than by use of the mirrors
- Vehicles with only a driver's seat
- Vehicles with more than eight passenger seats
- Loaded or partly loaded vehicles
- Vehicles over 3.5 tonnes in weight
- Vehicles towing trailers (For vehicles towing trailers see Part Three.)

You will lose your fee if the vehicle isn't suitable for the test.

Bribery

It is a criminal offence to attempt to bribe an examiner in any way.

This part looks at what the test requires.

The topics covered

- The eyesight test
- Theory into practice
- Before you start the engine
- The car controls
- Other controls
- Moving off
- Using the mirrors
- Giving signals
- Acting on signs and signals
- Controlling your speed
- Making progress
- The emergency stop
- Reversing around a corner
- Reverse parking
- Turning in the road
- Hazards
- Selecting a safe place to stop
- Awareness and anticipation

What the test requires

You must satisfy your examiner that, in good daylight, you can read a vehicle number plate with letters 79.4 mm (3.1 in.) high at a **minimum distance** of 20.5 metres (about 67 feet).

If you need glasses or contact lenses to read the number plate, that is fine. However, you must wear them during the test and whenever you drive or ride.

If you have had sight correction surgery you should declare this when you apply for your provisional licence.

How your examiner will test you

Before you get into your car your examiner will point out a vehicle and ask you to read its number plate.

If you can't speak English or have difficulty reading, you may copy down what you see.

If your answer is incorrect, your examiner will measure the exact distance and repeat the test.

If you fail the eyesight test

If you can't show your examiner that your eyesight is up to the required standard

- You will have failed your driving test
- Your test will go no further

N513 CTW

If you normally wear glasses or contact lenses, always wear them whenever you drive or ride.

What the test requires

You must satisfy your examiner that you have **fully understood** everything which you learned for the theory test.

The aspects are

- Alertness and concentration

- Courtesy and consideration

- Care in the use of the controls to reduce mechanical wear and tear

- Awareness of stopping distances and safety margins in all conditions

- Hazard awareness

- Correct action concerning pedestrians and other vulnerable road users

- Dealing with other types of vehicle in the correct manner

- Rules regarding speed limits and stopping restrictions

- Road and traffic signs

You will also be expected to know

- The law regarding you and your vehicle

- What to do in the event of an accident

- The effect extra loads have on your vehicle

How your examiner will test you

Your examiner will give you a few moments to get settled into your vehicle. She or he will then ask you to go ahead, unless you are asked to turn or the traffic signs direct you otherwise.

Throughout the test your examiner will expect you to demonstrate the knowledge you have gained by studying for your theory test.

Skills you should show

Steering

- Place your hands on the steering wheel in either the 'ten-to-two' or 'quarter-to-three' position, whichever is more comfortable
- Keep your steering movements steady and smooth
- When turning a corner, begin turning the wheel at the correct time

Faults you should avoid

Steering

Don't turn too early when steering around a corner. If you do, you risk

- Cutting the corner when turning right and putting other drivers at risk
- Striking the kerb when turning left

Don't turn too late. You could put other road users at risk by

- Swinging wide on left turns
- Overshooting right turns

Avoid

- Crossing your hands on the steering wheel
- Allowing the wheel to spin back after turning
- Resting your arm on the door

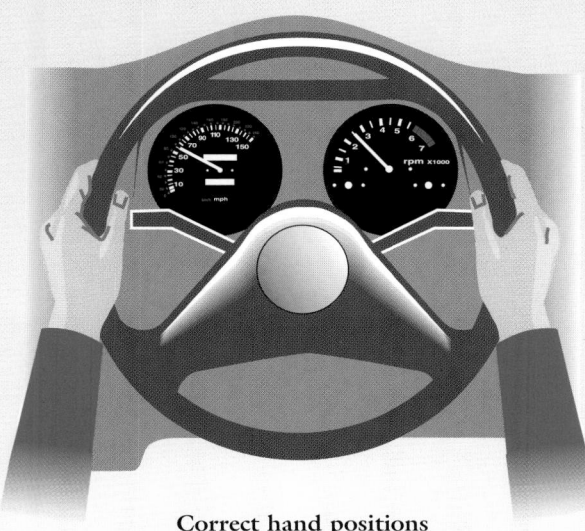

Correct hand positions for driving

You should understand

- The functions of all controls and switches which have a bearing on road safety
  - indicators
  - lights
  - windscreen wipers
  - demisters
  - heater

You should know where to find these controls on the vehicle you are driving.

- The meaning of gauges or other displays on the instrument panel
  - speedometer
  - various warning lights

Safety checks

You should also be able to carry out routine safety checks such as

- Oil and coolant levels
- Tyre pressures

In addition, you should be able to identify defects, especially with

- Steering
- Brakes
- Tyres
- Seat belts
- Lights
- Reflectors
- Horn
- Rear view mirrors
- Speedometer
- Exhaust system
- Direction indicators
- Windscreen wipers and washers

You should understand the effects which extra loads have on your vehicle such as

- A roof rack and luggage
- Extra passengers

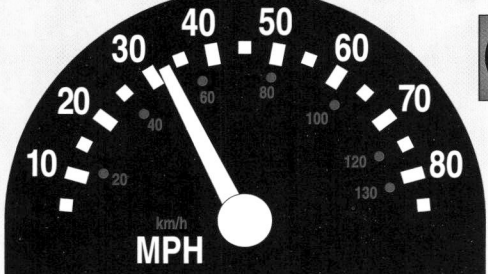

What the test requires

You should be able to move off

- Safely
- Under control
- On the flat
- From behind a parked car
- On a hill, where appropriate

How your examiner will test you

Your examiner will watch your

- Use of the controls each time you move off
- Observation of other road users

Skills you should show

Use your mirrors and signal if necessary.

Before you move off, look around over your shoulder and check any blind spots that can't be seen in your mirror. Check for

- Traffic
- Pedestrians

Move off under control making balanced use of the

- Accelerator
- Clutch
- Brakes
- Steering

You should also ensure that you move off in the correct gear.

Faults you should avoid

- Immediately signalling without effective observation around you
- Pulling out without looking
- Causing other road users to stop or alter their course
- Excessive acceleration
- Moving off in too high a gear
- Failing to co-ordinate the controls correctly and stalling the engine

What the test requires

Make sure that you use your mirrors effectively

- Before any manoeuvre
- To keep aware of what is happening behind you

Check carefully before

- Moving off
- Signalling
- Changing direction
- Turning to the left or right
- Overtaking or changing lanes
- Increasing speed
- Slowing down or stopping
- Opening your car door

How your examiner will test you

For this aspect of driving there is no special test. Your examiner will watch your use of mirrors as you drive.

Skills you should show

Use the Mirrors – Signal – Manoeuvre (MSM) routine. This is fully explained on page 37.

You should practise

- Looking before you signal
- Looking and signalling before you act
- Acting sensibly and safely on what you see in the mirrors

You should be aware that the mirrors won't show everything behind you.

Faults you should avoid

- Manoeuvring without looking in the mirrors
- Not acting on what you see when you look in the mirrors

**Act on what you see.
Just looking isn't enough.**

28

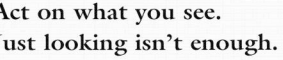

What the test requires

You should signal

- To let others know what you intend to do
- To help other road users, including pedestrians
- In plenty of time

You must only use the signals shown in *The Highway Code*.

Your signals should help other road users

- To understand what you intend to do
- To react safely

Always make sure that your signal is cancelled after use.

How your examiner will test you

For this aspect of the driving test there is no special exercise. Your examiner will watch carefully how you use your signals as you drive.

Skills you should show

Giving signals
- Clearly
- In good time

You should also know how to give arm signals and when they are necessary.

Faults you should avoid

- Giving signals carelessly
- Misleading other road users
- Forgetting to cancel the signal
- Waving at pedestrians to cross the road

What the test requires

You should be able to understand

- All traffic signs
- Road markings

React to them in good time.

At the beginning of the test your examiner will ask you to follow the road ahead.

You will be **asked** to turn at junctions, but look out for lane markings and direction signs. You will be expected to act on these.

Traffic lights

You must act correctly at traffic lights.

When the green light shows check that the road is clear before proceeding.

Signals by authorised persons

You must obey the signals given by

- Police officers
- Traffic wardens
- School crossing patrols

Traffic calming measures

Take extra care on roads which have been altered by the addition of

- 20 mph speed limit zones
- Speed restriction humps
- Width restrictions marked by bollards, posts or paved areas

GIVE WAY 50 yds

DSA THE DRIVING TEST

What the test requires

You should make good progress along the road bearing in mind

- Road conditions
- Traffic
- Weather
- Road signs and speed limits

How your examiner will test you

For this aspect of driving there is no special exercise. Your examiner will watch carefully your control of speed as you drive.

Skills you should show

You should

- Take great care in the use of speed
- Make sure that you can stop safely, well within the distance you can see to be clear
- Leave a safe distance between yourself and other vehicles
- Leave extra distance on wet or slippery roads
- Approach junctions and hazards at the correct speed

Faults you should avoid

- Driving too fast for the road and traffic conditions
- Changing your speed unpredictably

What the test requires

You should

- Make reasonable progress along the road
- Drive at a speed appropriate to road and traffic conditions
- Move off at junctions as soon as it safe to do so

How your examiner will test you

For this aspect of driving there is no special exercise. Your examiner will watch your driving and will want to see you

- Making reasonable progress along the road
- Keeping up with traffic
- Showing confidence, together with sound judgement
- Complying with the speed limits

Skills you should show

You should be able to choose the correct speed for the

- Type of road
- Type and density of traffic
- Weather and visibility

You should approach all hazards at a safe speed without

- Being too cautious
- Interfering with the progress of other traffic

Faults you should avoid

You shouldn't

- Drive too slowly, holding up other traffic
- Be over-cautious or stop and wait when it's safe to go
- Prepare too early for junctions by approaching too slowly and holding up traffic

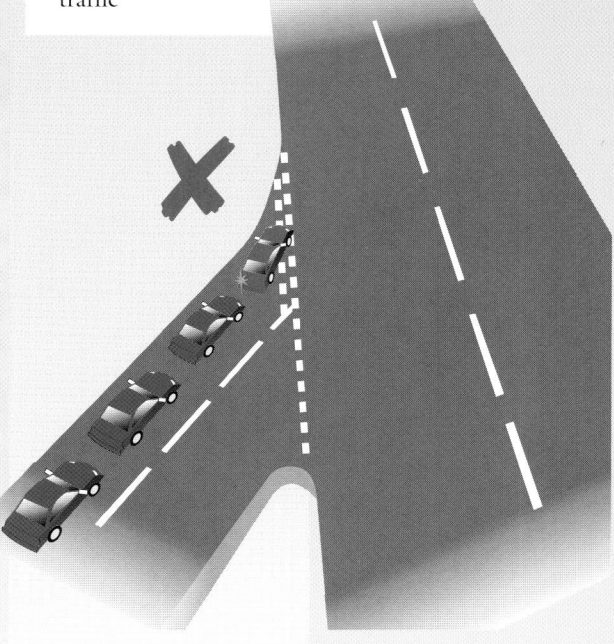

DSA THE DRIVING TEST

What the test requires

In an emergency you should be able to stop the car

- As quickly as possible
- Safely and under control
- Without locking the wheels

How your examiner will test you

Your examiner will

- Ask you to pull up on the side of the road
- Ask you to make an emergency stop when you are given the signal
- Demonstrate the signal to you

When your examiner gives the signal, try to stop the car as you would in a real emergency.

- You should react quickly
- Try to stop in a straight line

- Take special care if the road is wet

Your examiner will check that the road is clear behind you before the signal is given.

You might not be asked to do this exercise if you have to make a real emergency stop during the test.

Skills you should show

Stopping the car

- In a short distance
- Under full control
- Without risk to other road users

Faults you should avoid

- Anticipating the signal by stopping while your examiner is checking the road behind
- Skidding out of control
- Allowing the car to swing off course

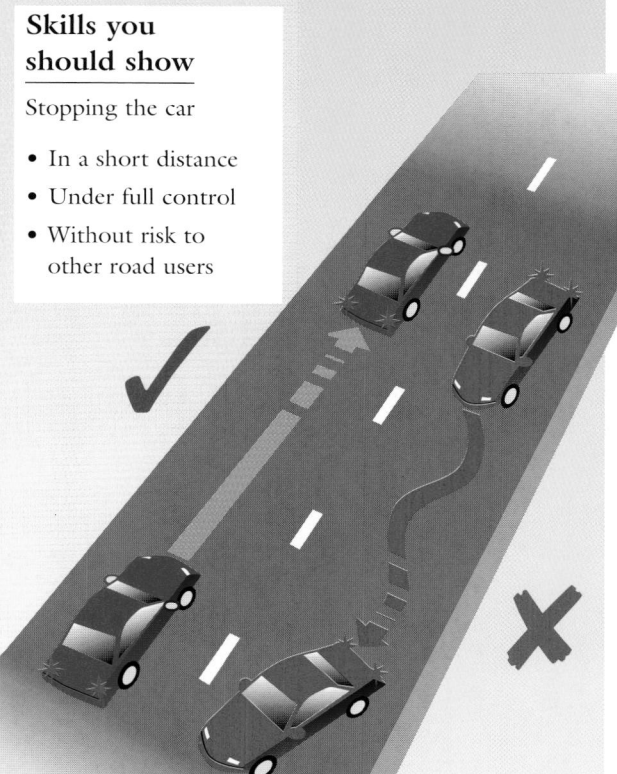

What the test requires

You should be able to reverse your car

- Smoothly
- Correctly
- Safely
- Under full control

How your examiner will test you

Your examiner will normally

- Ask you to pull up just before a side road on the left
- Point out the side road and ask you to reverse into it

You may undo your seat belt for the whole of the exercise. Do so only if it interferes with your driving. Don't forget to refasten it after you have completed the exercise.

If the view to the rear is restricted (in a van, for example) your examiner might ask you to reverse into a road on the right.

When your examiner asks you

- Make sure that you can carry out the exercise correctly and safely
- Check traffic and road conditions in all directions
- Reverse around the corner keeping a good lookout for traffic or pedestrians
- Straighten up your car and continue to reverse for a reasonable distance
- Pull up in a safe position and wait for your examiner's next instruction

Your car will swing out at the front as you reverse around the corner. Keep a good lookout for other road users.

Skills you should show

- Reversing under full control
- Keeping reasonably close to the kerb, without striking or mounting it
- Using good, effective all-round observation

Faults you should avoid

- Mounting the kerb
- Swinging out wide
- Reversing too far from the kerb
- Not showing consideration to other road users
- Taking more than a reasonable time to complete the exercise, creating a hazard for other road users
- Steering harshly while the car is stationary

DSA THE DRIVING TEST

What the test requires

You should be able to park your car safely at the kerb by reversing into the space of about two car lengths.

How your examiner will test you

When your examiner points out a parked car and asks you to park behind it

- Drive alongside the parked car and position your car so that you can carry out the exercise correctly and safely

- Select reverse gear – your reversing lights might help others to understand your intention

Use good, all-round observation and

- Reverse into the space behind the parked car, **within** the space of about two car lengths

- Stop reasonably close to and parallel with the kerb

Skills you should show

- Reversing under full control, safely and steadily

- Using good, effective all-round observation while reversing

Faults you should avoid

- Getting too close to the parked car

- Mounting the kerb

- Swinging your car from side to side

- Parking too far from the kerb or at an angle

- Not showing consideration or causing danger to other road users

- Taking more than a reasonable time to complete the exercise, causing an obstruction for other road users

- Steering harshly while the car is stationary

Keep a good lookout for traffic and pedestrians all the time.

What the test requires

You should be able to turn your car around in the road

- So that it faces in the opposite direction
- Using the forward and reverse gears

This will take at least three moves.

How your examiner will test you

Your examiner will

- Indicate a suitable place and ask you to pull up
- Ask you to turn your car around in the road

You should

- Make sure that the road is clear in both directions
- Drive forward in first gear turning the steering wheel to the right as much as possible

- Steer briskly to the left just before you pull up close to the opposite kerb
- Check all around, especially your blind spots
- Reverse, turning your steering wheel to the left as much as possible
- Steer briskly to the right before you pull up close to the kerb behind you
- Repeat if necessary until your car is facing in the opposite direction

Skills you should show

You should control your car smoothly. Make proper use of the

- Accelerator
- Clutch
- Brakes
- Steering

Show awareness of other road users. All-round observation is essential throughout the manoeuvre.

Faults you should avoid

- Mounting the kerb (try not to touch it)
- Not showing consideration or causing danger to other road users
- Taking more than a reasonable time to complete the exercise, causing an obstruction for other road users
- Steering harshly while the car is stationary

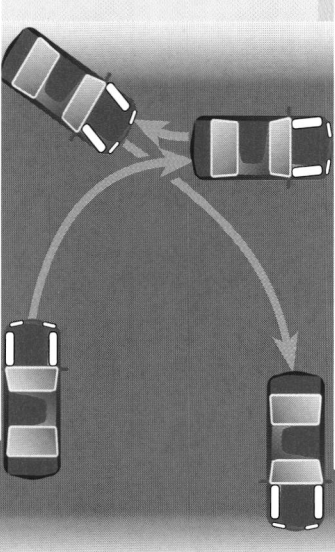

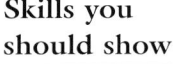

What is a hazard?

A hazard is any situation which could involve adjusting speed or altering course.

Look well ahead where there are

- Road junctions or roundabouts
- Parked vehicles
- Cyclists or horse riders
- Pedestrian crossings

By identifying the hazard early you will have time to take the appropriate action.

You may have to deal with several hazards at once or during a short space of time. This may mean using your initiative and common sense to deal with the particular circumstances.

What the test requires

Mirrors – Signal – Manoeuvre (MSM routine)

Always use this routine when approaching a hazard.

M – Mirrors

Check the position of traffic around and behind you.

S – Signal

Signal your intention to change course or slow down. Signal in good time.

M – Manoeuvre

A manoeuvre is any change of speed or position, from slowing or stopping the car to turning off a busy road.

What the test requires

You should

- Use the MSM routine when you approach a junction or a roundabout
- Position your car correctly. Adjust your speed and stop if necessary
- If the road has lane markings, use the correct lane. In a one-way street choose that lane as soon as you can do so safely

If the road has no lane markings, when turning left, keep to the left.

Watch out for

- Motorcyclists
- Cyclists
- Pedestrians crossing

When turning right

- Keep as close to the centre of the road as is safe
- Use effective observation before you enter a junction

How your examiner will test you

For this aspect of driving there is no special exercise. Your examiner will watch carefully and take account of your

- Use of the MSM routine
- Position and speed on approach
- Observation and judgement

DSA THE DRIVING TEST

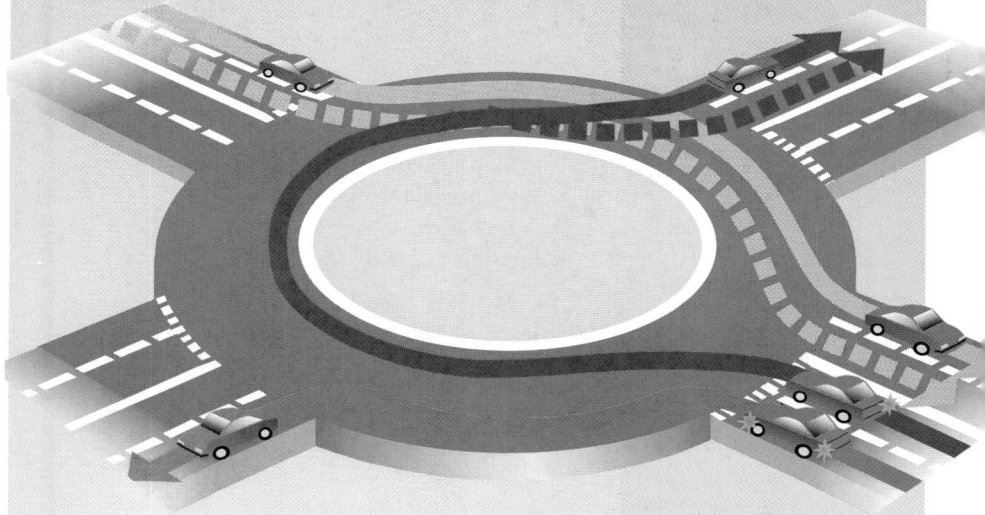

Skills you should show

You should be able to

- Observe road signs and markings and act correctly on what you see
- Judge the correct speed on approach
- Slow down in good time, without harsh braking
- Judge the speed of the other traffic, especially at roundabouts and when you are joining major roads

Faults you should avoid

- Approaching the junction at the wrong speed
- Positioning and turning incorrectly
- Stopping or waiting unnecessarily
- Entering a junction unsafely

What the test requires

When overtaking you must

- Allow enough room
- Give motorcyclists, cyclists and horses at least as much room as a car. They might swerve or wobble suddenly
- Allow enough space after overtaking. Don't cut in

Don't overtake

- If the road is narrow
- When your view is limited
- Where signs or road markings prohibit overtaking

How your examiner will test you

For this aspect of driving there is no special exercise. Your examiner will watch and take into account your

- Use of the MSM routine
- Reactions to road and traffic conditions
- Handling of the controls

Skills you should show

You should be able to judge the speed and position of vehicles

- Just behind, which might be trying to overtake you
- Just in front, if you are planning to overtake
- Coming towards you

Overtake only when you can do so

- Safely
- Without causing other vehicles to slow down or alter course

Faults you should avoid

You shouldn't overtake when

- Your view of the road ahead isn't clear
- You would have to exceed the speed limit

What the test requires

You should deal with oncoming traffic safely and confidently. This applies

- On narrow roads
- Where there are parked cars or other obstructions

If there is an obstruction on your side of the road, or not enough space for two vehicles to pass safely

- Use the MSM routine
- Be prepared to give way to oncoming traffic

If you need to stop, keep well back from the obstruction to give yourself

- A better view of the road ahead
- Room to move off easily when the road is clear

When you are passing parked cars, allow at least the width of a car door, if possible.

How your examiner will test you

For this aspect of driving there is no special exercise. Your examiner will watch carefully and take into account your

- Use of the MSM routine
- Reactions to road and traffic conditions
- Handling of the controls

Skills you should show

You should

- Show judgement and control when meeting oncoming traffic
- Be decisive when stopping and moving off
- Allow enough room when passing parked cars

Watch out for

- Doors opening
- Children running out into the road
- Pedestrians stepping out from the pavement
- Vehicles pulling out without warning

What the test requires

You should be able to cross the path of other vehicles safely and with confidence.

Crossing the path of other vehicles occurs mainly when you have to turn right into a side road or driveway. You should

- Use the MSM routine
- Position your car correctly and adjust your speed
- Keep as close to the centre of the road as is safe
- Watch out for oncoming traffic and stop if necessary

Watch out for pedestrians

- Crossing the side road
- On the pavement, if you are entering a driveway

If you are stopping behind another vehicle in a queue of traffic, leave enough room to pull out if the car in front breaks down.

How your examiner will test you

For this aspect of driving there is no special exercise. Your examiner will watch carefully and take account of your judgement of the oncoming traffic.

Skills you should show

You should show that you can turn right into a junction or driveway safely by using the MSM routine.

Faults you should avoid

Causing other vehicles to

- Slow down
- Swerve
- Stop

You shouldn't

- Cut the corner
- Go beyond the correct turning point before you begin to turn

What the test requires

You should always drive so that you can stop in the distance you can see to be clear.

Always keep a safe distance between you and the vehicle in front.

In good conditions, leave a gap of at least 1 metre (just over 3 feet) for every mile per hour you are travelling. Or, leave a two-second time gap.

In bad conditions, leave at least double the distance or a four-second time gap.

In slow-moving, congested traffic it may not be practical to leave as much space.

How your examiner will test you

For this aspect of driving there is no special exercise. Your examiner will watch carefully and take account of your

- Use of the MSM routine
- Anticipation
- Reaction to changing road and traffic conditions
- Handling of the controls

Skills you should show

You should

- Be able to judge a safe separation distance between you and the vehicle in front
- Show correct use of the MSM routine, especially before reducing speed
- Avoid the need to brake harshly if the vehicle in front slows down or stops
- Take extra care when your view ahead is limited by large vehicles such as lorries or buses

Watch out for

- Brake lights ahead
- Direction indicators
- Vehicles ahead braking without warning

Faults you should avoid

- Following too closely
- Braking suddenly
- Stopping too close to the vehicle in front in a traffic queue

What the test requires

You should

- Normally keep well to the left
- Keep clear of parked vehicles
- Avoid weaving in and out between parked vehicles
- Position your vehicle correctly for the direction you intend to take

You should obey all lane markings, especially

- Left- or right-turn arrows at junctions
- When approaching roundabouts
- In one-way streets
- Bus and cycle lanes

How your examiner will test you

For this aspect of driving there is no special exercise. Your examiner will watch carefully to see that you

- Use the MSM routine
- Select the correct lane in good time

Skills you should show

You should

- Plan ahead and choose the correct lane in good time
- Use the MSM routine correctly
- Position your vehicle sensibly, even if there are no road markings

Faults you should avoid

- Driving too close to the kerb
- Driving too close to the centre of the road
- Changing lanes at the last moment or without good reason
- Hindering other road users by being badly positioned or being in the wrong lane
- Straddling lanes or lane markings
- Cutting across the path of other traffic in another lane at roundabouts

DSA THE DRIVING TEST

What the test requires

You should

- Recognise the different types of pedestrian crossing
- Show courtesy and consideration towards pedestrians
- Stop safely when necessary

At all pedestrian crossings

You should slow down and stop if there is anyone on the crossing.

At zebra crossings

You should

- Slow down and be prepared to stop if there is anyone waiting to cross
- Know how to give the correct arm signal, if necessary, before slowing down or stopping

At pelican, puffin and toucan crossings

You must

- Stop if the lights are red
- Give way to any pedestrians on a pelican crossing when the amber lights are flashing
- Give way to cyclists on a toucan crossing, as you would to pedestrians

How your examiner will test you

For this aspect of driving there is no special exercise. Your examiner will watch carefully and take account of how you deal with pedestrian crossings.

Skills you should show

You should be able to

- Approach a pedestrian crossing at a controlled speed
- Stop safely when necessary
- Move off when it's safe, keeping a good lookout

Faults you must avoid

- Approaching a crossing too fast
- Driving over a crossing without stopping or showing awareness of waiting pedestrians
- Blocking a crossing by stopping directly on it

Don't hurry pedestrians by

- Sounding the horn
- Revving the engine
- Edging forward

Don't

- Overtake within the zigzag white lines leading up to crossings
- Wave pedestrians across
- Take late or incorrect action on traffic light signals at controlled crossings

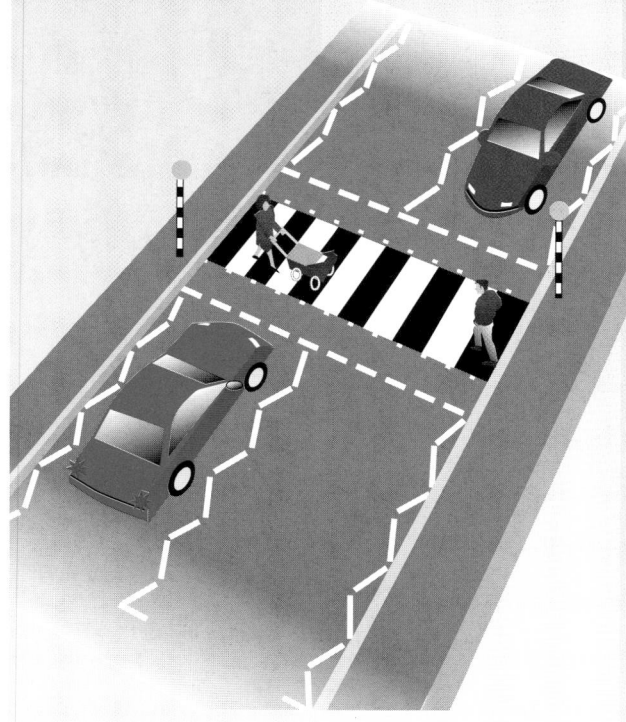

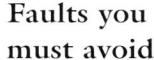

DSA THE DRIVING TEST

Faults you should avoid

- Reacting suddenly to road or traffic conditions rather than anticipating them
- Showing irritation with other road users
- Sounding the horn aggressively
- Revving your engine or edging forward when waiting for pedestrians to cross a road

This part looks at what is required when towing a trailer.

The topics covered

- Before the test
- The reversing exercise
- The braking exercise
- The drive
- Uncoupling and recoupling

Cars towing trailers or caravans

You must pass a category B theory and practical test before towing a trailer in this category.

If you want to tow a large trailer and you don't hold a full driving licence issued before 1 January 1997 you may have to take a further test (category B + E).

The booklet INS 57, enclosed with your provisional licence, or DVLA factsheet INF 30 'Towing Trailers in Great Britain' will give you the full information.

When you practise

When you practise you must

- Display L plates (or if you wish, D plates in Wales) front and rear. These must be clearly visible
- Have with you a person who has held and still holds a licence for category B + E for three years. They must be 21 years or over

How and where to practise

- On as many different roads as you can
- In all sorts of traffic conditions

Practise reversing your vehicle and trailer. You will be given a reversing exercise during your test. When you practise, try not to obstruct other traffic.

You should practise turning left and right, taking into consideration the extra length of the unit. Be aware of your trailer when taking sharp turns.

Practise uncoupling and recoupling your vehicle and trailer. You will be asked to demonstrate this at the end of your test.

If you wish to take a category B + E test, the trailer you use for the test must be at least 1 tonne Maximum Authorised Mass (MAM).

The officially recommended syllabus for learning to drive vehicles with trailers (category B + E) can be found on pages 84–6.

Further information and advice on towing trailers can be found in *The Driving Manual* (The Stationery Office).

The test will include an eyesight test. You must be able to read a number plate with letters 79.4 mm (3.1 in.) high from 20.5 metres (about 67 feet).

If you need glasses or contact lenses to read the number plate, you must wear them when you are driving.

Your driving licence

Make sure that you have your full licence with you and that you have signed it. Any of the following licences are acceptable

- A full licence issued in Great Britain (GB)
- A full licence issued in Northern Ireland (NI)

Your examiner might not be able to conduct your test if you can't produce one of these documents.

Your test vehicle

Make sure that the vehicle you intend to drive during your test is

- Legally roadworthy and has a current test certificate, if it's over three years old
- Fully covered by insurance for its present use and for you to drive. Your examiner will ask you to sign a declaration that your insurance is in order. The test won't be conducted if you are unable to do so

- Properly licenced with a valid tax disc displayed
- Displaying L plates (or if you wish, D plates in Wales) to the front of your vehicle and the rear of your trailer. They shouldn't be displayed on the windscreen. Both you and your examiner must have a clear view of the road

Make sure that the trailer you intend to tow is

- Legally roadworthy
- At least 1 tonne Maximum Authorised Mass (MAM)

If you overlook any of these

- Your test may be cancelled
- You could lose your fee

DSA THE DRIVING TEST

What the test requires

There is no emergency stop exercise in the category B + E test.

For safety reasons, the braking exercise will take place on a special manoeuvring area and not on the public roads. Your examiner will be with you in the vehicle for this exercise.

She or he will point out two marker cones approximately 61 metres (200 feet) ahead. You should build up a speed of about 20 mph. When the front of the vehicle passes between the two markers you should apply the brakes. You should stop your vehicle and trailer with safety and under full control.

Skills you should show

You should stop the vehicle

- As quickly as possible
- Under full control
- As safely as possible
- In a straight line

20 mph

Start

Faults you should avoid

- Driving too slowly (less than 20 mph)
- Braking too soon (anticipating the marker points)
- Braking too harshly, causing skidding
- Depressing the clutch too late (stalling the engine)
- Taking too long to stop

What the test requires

Your examiner will expect you to drive to a standard at least that of the driving test for category B.

The test will be approximately one hour's duration. It will include a wide variety of roads and traffic conditions.

The route will take in roads carrying two-way traffic, dual carriageways and, where possible, one-way systems.

You will be expected to demonstrate that you can move off smoothly and safely both uphill and downhill. You will also have to move off normally from the side of the road and at an angle.

You won't be required to carry out the following exercises

- Emergency stop on the road
- Reversing around a corner
- Reverse parking
- Turning in the road

Skills you should show

You will need to show that you can safely

- Meet other vehicles
- Overtake
- Cross the path of other vehicles
- Keep a safe separation distance
- Negotiate various types of roundabout
- Exercise correct lane discipline
- Display courtesy and consideration to other road users especially

  – pedestrians

  – riders on horseback

  – cyclists

  – motorcyclists

- Apply the correct procedure at

  – pedestrian crossings

  – level crossings

  – traffic signals

  – road junctions

You will need to show

- Effective use of the mirrors
- Correct use of signals
- Alertness and anticipation
- Correct use of speed
- Observation of speed limits
- Care in the use of the controls to reduce mechanical wear and tear

Fault you should avoid

- Not using good, all-round observation to ensure that your vehicle and trailer negotiate hazards and junctions safely

What the test requires

When uncoupling you should

- Ensure that the brakes are applied on both the vehicle and the trailer. (Extra care should be taken in the case of an ALCO chassis as the anti-reverse mechanism needs to be overcome.)

- Ensure that the jockey wheel is lowered correctly

- Disconnect the electric line(s) and stow away safely

- Remove any fitted stabilising equipment

- Remove any safety chain or coupling

- Release the coupling and move the trailer clear of the towing hook

- Pull forward approximately one vehicle length

When recoupling you should

- Move the towing vehicle so that the trailer can be safely and easily coupled to it, and apply the parking brake

- Attach the trailer to the towing vehicle and check that the coupling is secure by using a method appropriate to the vehicle and trailer

- Attach any safety chain or device

- Fit any necessary stabilising equipment

- Connect the electric line(s)

- Ensure that the wheels, legs or other supporting devices are raised and secured safely

- Release the trailer brake, ensuring that the handbrake of the towing vehicle is firmly applied

- Check the operation of the lights and indicators

If you have a disability which makes it difficult to complete this exercise, please state this on your application form.

How your examiner will test you

You will normally be asked to uncouple and recouple your vehicle and trailer at the test centre at end of the test.

Your examiner will ask you to

- Stop where there is safe and level ground
- Demonstrate the uncoupling of your vehicle and trailer
- Pull forward approximately one vehicle length
- Reverse the vehicle up to the trailer
- Recouple the vehicle and trailer

Your examiner will expect you to make sure that the

- Coupling is secure
- Lights and indicators are operating
- Trailer brake is released

Skills you should show

You should be able to uncouple and recouple your vehicle and trailer

- In the correct sequence (order)
- Confidently and in good time

DSA THE DRIVING TEST

Faults you should avoid

When uncoupling

- Starting the uncoupling without applying the brakes on both the vehicle and the trailer
- Releasing the trailer coupling without the wheels or legs lowered
- Moving forward before the entire correct procedure has been completed

When recoupling

- Not checking the brakes are applied on the trailer
- Not using good, effective observation
- Recoupling at speed

Don't attempt to move away without

- Raising the wheels or legs
- Checking

  - lights

  - indicators

  - safety chain

  - trailer brake release

PART FOUR THE MOTORCYCLE TEST

This part looks at what the test requires
when riding a motorcycle.

The topics covered

- Preparation and training
- Compulsory Basic Training (CBT)
- The test

Motorcycle and moped riders

To ride a motorcycle on the road you must

- Be at least 17 years of age

- Have a driving licence which allows you to ride motorcycles (category A)

To ride a moped on the road you must

- Be at least 16 years of age

- Have a licence which allows you to ride mopeds (category P)

The licences can be any of the following

- Full motorcycle licence

- Full car licence. This provides automatic provisional motorcycle entitlement

- Full moped licence. This provides automatic provisional motorcycle entitlement if you are aged 17 or over

- A provisional driving licence with motorcycle entitlement

You must wear a safety helmet at all times when riding, unless you are a member of the Sikh religion and wear a turban.

If your helmet has a visor it must conform to the required BSI standard.

Compulsory Basic Training (CBT)

Learner motorcyclists and moped riders must complete a CBT course before riding on the road. This includes riders who hold a

- Full car licence and are riding on the provisional entitlement this provides

- Provisional driving licence with motorcycle entitlement

When you have completed a CBT course you will be given a Certificate of Completion (DL196). Keep this safe. You must have a DL196 before you can take the motorcycle test.

You don't have to take CBT if you

- Have passed a full moped test after 1 December 1990

- Live and ride on specified offshore islands

- Already hold a valid Certificate of Completion (DL196), obtained during a previous motorcycling entitlement or when riding a moped

Since 1 July 1996 CBT certificates have a three-year life. This includes

- Certificates issued before this date. Those certificates will have a three-year life from 1 July 1996

- Certificates issued on or after this date. Those will have a three-year life from their date of issue

Provisional motorcycle entitlement

This entitles learners to ride a solo motorcycle of up to 125cc with a maximum power output of 11kW. Learners who wish to ride a side-car outfit can do so with a power to weight ratio not exceeding 0.16kW/kg. If you aren't sure, ask for advice from your motorcycle dealer.

With provisional motorcycle entitlement you must not

- Ride on motorways
- Carry a pillion passenger
- Ride without L plates (or if you wish, D plates in Wales)

Two-year limit

The motorcycle entitlement on a provisional licence lasts for two years. You must pass the motorcycle test within that time or your entitlement will expire. You will then have to wait one year before you can apply for motorcycle entitlement again.

Types of licence

Light motorcycle licence

If you pass your test on a motorcycle of between 75 and 125cc you will obtain a full light motorcycle licence. This will provide full licence entitlement on any motorcycle up to 125cc and with a power output of up to 11kW (14.6 bhp). If your test machine is between 120 and 125cc AND capable of 100 kph, you will attain a full standard motorcycle licence.

Standard motorcycle licence

Your test motorcycle must be over 120cc but no larger than 125cc. It must be capable of at least 100 kph. Your full standard motorcycle licence will be subject to the two-year qualifying period.

If you pass your test on a motorcycle with an automatic or semi-automatic transmission, this will be recorded on your licence. Your full licence entitlement will be restricted to motorcycles in this category.

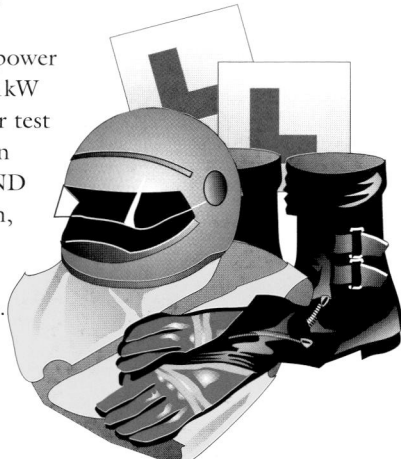

Two-year qualifying period

After obtaining the full standard motorcycle licence (category A) you may

- Ride on motorways
- Carry a pillion passenger
- Ride without L plates (or if you wish, D plates in Wales)

However, you are restricted to motorcycles of up to 25kW (33 bhp) for two years. After two years you may ride any size of motorcycle without taking another test.

Accelerated access

The accelerated access option is for riders who are 21 years or over, or reach the age of 21 before their two-year qualifying period is complete.

Those riders can take a further test to give them immediate access to all motorcycles. This test must be taken on a motorcycle with a power output of at least 35kW (46.6 bhp).

Riders may practise for this test on motorcycles above 25kW provided

- They are accompanied at all times by an Approved Instructor, on another motorcycle and in radio contact
- Fluorescent or reflective safety clothing is worn during supervision
- L plates (or if you wish, D plates in Wales) are fitted and provisional licence restrictions followed

Direct access

This option is open to learner riders aged 21 or over. Such riders can take one test to give them direct access to any size of motorcycle. However, they will have to take a CBT course before riding on the road.

Riders may practise on any size of motorcycle, but the test must be taken on a motorcycle of at least 35kW (46.6 bhp).

If you practise on a motorcycle which exceeds 125cc you must

- Be accompanied at all times by an Approved Instructor, on another motorcycle and in radio contact
- Wear fluorescent or reflective safety clothing during supervision
- Have fitted L plates (or if you wish, D plates in Wales) to your machine
- Follow provisional licence restrictions

Element A: Introduction

Before you do any practical training you should understand

- The aims of the CBT course
- The importance of the right equipment and clothing
- The need to be clearly visible to other road users
- The legal requirements when riding on the road
- Why motorcyclists and moped riders are more vulnerable than other road users
- The need to ride at the correct speed according to road and traffic conditions
- The importance of reading and understanding *The Highway Code*

Eyesight

Your eyesight will be tested and you must be able to read a number plate

- In good daylight
- Containing letters and figures 79.4 mm (3.1 in.) high
- At a distance of 20.5 metres (about 67 feet)
- With the aid of glasses or contact lenses if you normally wear them

Element B: Practical on-site training

This element gives you an introduction to your motorcycle. It will help you to become familiar with the motorcycle, its controls and how it works. At the end of this element you will have demonstrated your ability to

- Carry out basic machine checks
- Take the motorcycle on and off its stand
- Wheel the motorcycle around to the left and right, showing proper balance
- Bring the motorcycle to a halt by braking
- Start and stop the engine satisfactorily

Element E: Practical on-road riding

For this final element you will go out on the road with your instructor for a minimum of two hours, possibly with another trainee. You will have to demonstrate that you can ride competently and safely in a variety of road and traffic conditions. Your training will include as many of the following as possible

- Traffic lights
- Roundabouts
- Junctions
- Pedestrian crossings
- Gradients
- Bends
- Obstructions

The Certificate of Completion

When you have satisfactorily completed Element E you will be given a Certificate of Completion of Approved Training Course (DL196). This will have a three-year life from its date of issue.

This certificate validates the provisional motorcycle entitlement on your driving licence. With the DL196 you are now licensed to ride on the road and to practise for your motorcycle or moped test.

Talk to your approved training body about taking further training to prepare you for the test.

Present the DL196 to your driving examiner when you attend the test. It is important that you remember this, otherwise your test will be cancelled and you could lose your fee.

Special features

You should read Parts One and Two of this book. Most of the information given there will apply to you. You will have to take and pass the theory test before you take the practical test (see page 5).

Some extra requirements are

Emergency stop

You need to

- Apply the front brake just before the rear
- Apply both brakes effectively
- Stop the machine as quickly as possible without locking either wheel

Walking with your machine

Your examiner will ask you to put your machine on its stand. You will then be asked to remove the machine from its stand and to walk with it, but without the aid of the engine.

Riding a U-turn

Your examiner will then ask you to ride back in a U-turn. Direct rear observation into the blind area is vital just before you carry out the manoeuvre.

Angle start

Your examiner will ask you to pull up just before a parked vehicle. Before you move off, make sure that you check

- To the rear and into the blind area
- Ahead to see there is no danger from approaching traffic

If an angle start occurs normally during the test you may not be asked to do it again.

Slow ride

You will be asked to ride along at a walking speed for a short distance. This exercise tests your control, balance and observation. If you have already ridden slowly, such as in traffic, you may not be asked to carry out this exercise.

Hill start

Your examiner might ask you to pull up on an uphill gradient. When moving off, your machine could be slower accelerating. You will need to remember this when judging the moment to ride off.

DSA THE DRIVING TEST

How your examiner will test you

Before the test you will be fitted with

- Earphones under your helmet
- A radio receiver on a waist belt

When you are taking the test your examiner will follow you either on a motorcycle or in a car. Before the emergency stop exercise your examiner will stand next to you and give you your instructions.

Your test will be carried out over a route covering a wide variety of road and traffic conditions.

At the end of the test your examiner will ask you a question about carrying pillion passengers on your machine.

This part looks at what is required when
being tested after disqualification.

The topic covered

* The extended test

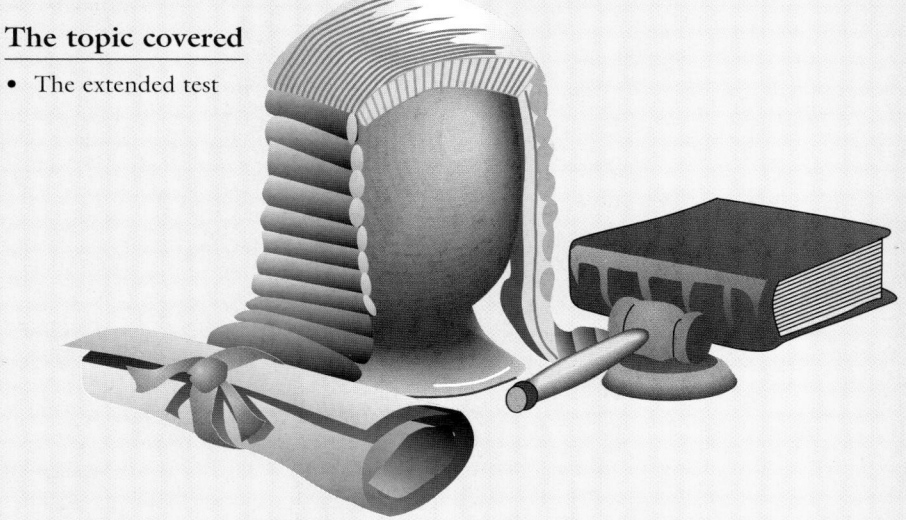

Penalties

Tough penalties exist for anyone convicted of dangerous driving offences.

Courts can

- Impose an extended driving test on anyone convicted of dangerous driving offences

- Impose an extended driving test on anyone convicted of other offences involving obligatory disqualification

- Order a normal-length test for other endorsable offences before the disqualified driver or rider can recover a full licence

Applying for a retest

A driver subject to a retest can apply for a provisional licence at the end of the disqualification period.

The normal rules for provisional licence-holders apply.

The driver must be supervised by a person who

- Has held a full driving licence for at least three years and still holds one for the category of the vehicle being driven

- Is at least 21 years of age

The vehicle must display L plates or, if you wish, D plates if being driven in Wales, to the front and rear.

Driving on motorways isn't allowed.

Mopeds and motorcycles

A rider subject to a retest can apply for a provisional licence at the end of the disqualification period.

The normal rules for provisional licence-holders apply

- L plates or, if you wish, D plates if riding in Wales, must be displayed to the front and rear of the machine
- Solo motorcycles must not exceed 125cc and 11kW power output (unless riding under the direct access scheme)
- Riding on motorways isn't allowed

In addition, riders should check whether they have to take a CBT course before riding on the road with their provisional licence.

For further information, contact your nearest DSA Area Office.

The theory test

You will have to pass the theory test before an application for the practical test is accepted.

Details of the theory test can be found in Part One.

Longer and more demanding

The extended test takes about 70 minutes and covers a wide variety of roads, usually including dual carriageways. This test is more demanding. Make sure that you are ready.

You are advised to take suitable instruction from an ADI.

Higher fees

The fee reflects the length of the test.

How your examiner will test you

Your test will include all the exercises included in the normal test. Your examiner will watch you and take account of

- Your ability to concentrate for the duration of the test
- Your attitude to other road users

This part offers further information.

The topics covered

- If you pass
- The *Pass Plus* scheme
- If you don't pass
- Officially recommended syllabus
- DSA complaints guide for test candidates
- DSA compensation code for test candidates
- DSA offices and other useful addresses

If you pass

Well done! Your passing the driving test will have shown that you can drive safely.

You will be given

- A pass certificate (D10, or a D10E in the case of an extended test)
- A copy of the driving test report which will show any minor faults which have been marked during the test*

Look at the report carefully and discuss it with your instructor. This is given to you to help you to overcome any weaknesses in your driving.

* Note: Motorcycle test candidates will only be given a pass certificate (form D10 or D10E).

Developing your driving standards

You should aim to raise your standard of driving with additional instruction and experience.

The *Pass Plus* scheme has been developed by the Department of Transport, in partnership with the insurance industry, to enable you to gain experience safely. Your instructor may have details, or you may contact the DSA Head Office for the names of instructors operating in your area.

You may also wish to contact voluntary organisations such as

- The Guild of Experienced Motorists (GEM)
- The Institute of Advanced Motorists (IAM)
- The Royal Society for the Prevention of Accidents (RoSPA)

Motorway driving

It is important that you understand the rules and regulations of the motorway. Your ADI will be able to assist you with gaining some experience before you drive on your own. This will help you to gain the confidence you will need to drive on a busy motorway.

Ask your ADI for lessons in motorway driving.

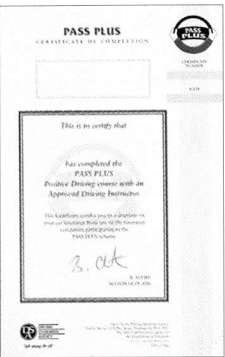

Pass Plus

Pass Plus is a training scheme linked to insurance discounts that will benefit you, the **newly qualified driver** by

- Saving you money on your car insurance premiums
- Showing you a positive driving style which is both enjoyable and safe
- Helping you to gain quality driving experience safely

The *Pass Plus* scheme has been developed by the Department of Transport with the help of insurers and the driver instruction industry.

The scheme has been developed to

- Improve your skills in areas where you may have little experience
- Reduce your risk of being involved in a road accident

You will have to pay for the course but, if you complete it successfully, you will be offered a discount on your car insurance by one of the companies taking part in the scheme. The precise saving will depend on the company you choose.

Fees for the *Pass Plus* course will vary depending on where you live and the instructor or driving school you choose.

By choosing to take part in the scheme you will have shown that you want to be a skilful and responsible driver.

The aim of the *Pass Plus* scheme

The *Pass Plus* scheme will

- Speed up the process of gaining good driving experience
- Teach you positive driving skills

Throughout the course you will be driving with two key factors in mind

Attitude

- Responsibility for your actions
- Care and consideration for others

Skills

- Observation
- Assessing what you see
- Making decisions
- Taking the right action

Your instructor will tell you why they are the key to a **positive driving** style.

DSA THE DRIVING TEST

Driving is a life skill. It will take you many years to acquire the skills set out here to a high standard.

This syllabus lists the skills in which you must achieve basic competence in order to pass the driving test. You must also have

- A thorough knowledge of *The Highway Code* and motoring laws

- A thorough understanding of your responsibilities as a driver

This means that you must have real concern, not just for your own safety but for the safety of all road users, including pedestrians.

Make sure that your instructor covers the syllabus fully.

Legal requirements

To learn to drive you must

1. Be at least 17 years old. If you receive a mobility allowance for a disability you may start driving at 16

2. Be able to read in good daylight (with glasses or contact lenses, if you wear them) a motor vehicle number plate

– 20.5 metres (about 67 feet) away

– with letters 79.4 mm (3.1 in.) high

3. Be medically fit to drive

4. Hold a provisional driving licence or full licence for another category (see leaflet D100)*

5. Ensure that the vehicle being driven

– is legally roadworthy

– has a current test certificate if it's over the prescribed age

– displays a valid tax disc

6. Make sure that the vehicle is properly insured for its use

7. Display L plates or, if you wish, D plates in Wales, to the front and rear of the vehicle

8. Be supervised by a person who

– has held (and still holds) a full licence for the category of vehicle driven for at least three years

– is at least 21 years old

9. Wear a seat belt, unless granted an exemption, and see that all the seat belts in the vehicle and their anchorages and fitting are free from obvious defects

* Leaflet D100 contains general information on driver licensing and is free from the DVLA or post offices.

10. Ensure that children under 14 years are suitably restrained by the appropriate restraint or an adult seat belt

11. Be aware of the legal requirements to notify medical conditions which could affect safe driving. If a vehicle has been adapted for a disability, ensure that all the adaptations are suitable to control the vehicle safely

12. Know the rules on the issue, presentation or display of

– driving licences

– insurance certificates

– tax discs

Car controls, equipment and components

You must

1. Understand the function of the

– accelerator

– clutch

– gears

– footbrake

– handbrake

– steering

and be able to use these competently

2. Know the function of other controls and switches in the car that have a bearing on road safety, and use them competently

3. Understand the meaning of the gauges and other displays on the instrument panel

4. Know the legal requirements for the vehicle

5. Be able to carry out routine safety checks such as

– oil and coolant levels

– tyre pressures

and identify defects, especially with the

– steering

– brakes

– tyres

– seat belts

– lights

– reflectors

– direction indicators

– windscreen wipers and washers

– horn

– rear view mirrors

– speedometer

– exhaust system

6. Understand the effects which a loaded roof rack or extra passengers will have on the handling of your vehicle

Road user behaviour

You must

1. Know the most common causes of accidents

2. Know which road users are most at risk and how to reduce that risk

3. Know the rules, risks and effects of drinking and driving

4. Know the effect of fatigue, illness and drugs on driving performance

5. Be aware of any age-related problems among other road users, especially among children, teenagers and the elderly

DSA THE DRIVING TEST

6. Be alert and able to anticipate the likely actions of other road users, and be able to take appropriate precautions

7. Be aware that courtesy and consideration towards other road users are essential for safe driving

Vehicle characteristics

You must

1. Know the important principles concerning braking distances and road holding under various road and weather conditions

2. Know the handling characteristics of other vehicles with regard to stability, speed, braking and manoeuvrability

3. Know that some vehicles are less easily seen than others

4. Be able to assess the risks caused by the characteristics of other vehicles and suggest precautions that can be taken, for example

– large commercial vehicles pulling to the right before turning left

– blind spots for some commercial vehicle drivers

– bicycles and motorcycles being buffeted by strong winds

Road and weather conditions

You must

1. Know the particular hazards in both daylight and the dark, and on different types of road, for example

– on single carriageways, including country lanes

– on three-lane roads

– on dual carriageways and motorways

2. Gain driving experience on urban and higher-speed roads (but not on motorways) in both daylight and the dark

3. Know which road surfaces provide the better or poorer grip when braking

4. Know the hazards caused by bad weather, for example

– rain

– fog

– snow

– ice

– strong winds

5. Be able to assess the risks caused by road and traffic conditions, be aware of how the conditions may cause others to drive unsafely, and be able to take appropriate precautions

Traffic signs, rules and regulations

You must

1. Have sound knowledge of the meaning of traffic signs and road markings

2. Have a sound grasp of the meaning of traffic signs, for example

– speed limits

– parking restrictions

– zebra and pelican crossings

Car control and road procedure

You must have the knowledge and skills to carry out the following tasks safely and competently, practising the proper use of mirrors, observation and signals.

1. Take necessary precautions before getting in or out of the vehicle

2. Before starting the engine, carry out safety checks on

– doors

– seat and head restraints

– seat belts

– mirrors

Also check that the handbrake is on and the gear lever is in neutral

3. Start the engine and move off

– straight ahead and at an angle

– on the level, uphill and downhill

4. Select the correct road position for normal driving

5. Use proper observation in all traffic conditions

6. Drive at a speed suitable for road and traffic conditions

7. React promptly to all risks

8. Change traffic lanes

9. Pass stationary vehicles

10. Meet, overtake and cross the path of other vehicles

11. Turn right and left at junctions, including crossroads and roundabouts

12. Drive ahead at crossroads and roundabouts

13. Keep a safe separation distance when following other traffic

14. Act correctly at pedestrian crossings

15. Show proper regard for the safety of other road users, with particular care towards the most vulnerable

16. Drive on both urban and rural roads and, where possible, dual carriageways – keeping up with the flow of traffic where it's safe and proper to do so

17. Comply with traffic regulations and traffic signals given by the police, traffic wardens and other road users

18. Stop the vehicle safely, normally and in an emergency, without locking the wheels

You must achieve everything in the previous sections of this syllabus except items which clearly don't apply to you. In particular, you should know how to

1. Turn a vehicle and trailer to travel in the opposite direction without reversing, where possible. For example, using a roundabout or side roads

2. Stop the vehicle and trailer as quickly as possible, with safety and under full control

3. Reverse the towing vehicle and trailer

– under control

– with effective observation

– on a predetermined course

– to enter a restricted opening

– to stop so that the extreme rear of the trailer is within a clearly defined area

4. Select a safe and suitable place to stop the vehicle and trailer reasonably close to the nearside kerb when required

– on the level

– facing uphill

– facing downhill

– before reaching a parked vehicle, but leaving sufficient room to move away again

5. Use additional mirrors and observation to compensate for the restricted view caused by large trailers and caravans

6. Show consideration for other road users by pulling up safely, when necessary, to avoid the build-up of queues of following traffic

7. Uncouple and recouple the trailer from the towing vehicle safely

Uncoupling

You must

– select a safe place with firm and level ground

– ensure that the brakes are applied on both the towing vehicle and the trailer

– ensure that the wheels, legs or other devices provided for supporting the trailer after uncoupling are lowered correctly, and that strong planks or metal load spreaders are used to distribute the weight if there is any risk

– disconnect the electric line(s) and stow them away safely

– remove any chain or coupling and manoeuvre the trailer clear of the towing hook

– remove any fitted stabilising equipment and the trailer number plate, where appropriate

Recoupling

You must

– ensure that the brakes are correctly applied on the trailer

– manoeuvre the towing vehicle so that the trailer may be safely and easily coupled to it

– attach the vehicle to the towing vehicle securely

– attach any safety chain or device and the electrical connections

– correctly fit any stabilising equipment

– connect the electric line(s)

– ensure that the wheels, legs or other devices provided for supporting the trailer are raised and secured correctly

– check that the coupling is secure by using a method appropriate to the vehicle and trailer

– check the operation of all lights and the fitting of the correct number plate, where appropriate

– release the trailer brake, having ensured that the handbrake on the towing vehicle is on

DSA aims to give its customers the best possible service. Please tell us

- When we have done well
- When you aren't satisfied

Your comments can help us to improve the service we have to offer. For information about DSA service standards, contact your local Area Office.

If you have any questions about how your test was conducted, please contact the local Supervising Examiner, whose address is displayed at your local driving test centre. If you are dissatisfied with the reply or you wish to comment on other matters, you can write to the Area Manager (see the list of Area Offices at the back of this book).

If your concern relates to an ADI you should write to

The Registrar of Approved Driving Instructors Driving Standards Agency Stanley House Talbot Street Nottingham NG1 5GU

Finally, you can write to

The Chief Executive Driving Standards Agency Stanley House Talbot Street Nottingham NG1 5GU

None of this removes your right to take your complaint to

- Your Member of Parliament, who may decide to raise your case personally with the DSA Chief Executive, the Minister, or the Parliamentary Commissioner for Administration (the Ombudsman), whose name and address is at the back of this book

- A magistrates court (in Scotland, to the Sheriff of your area) if you believe that your test wasn't carried out according to the regulations

Before doing this, **you should seek legal advice.**

DSA always aims to keep test appointments, but occasionally we have to cancel a test at short notice. We will refund the test fee, or give you your next test free, in the following circumstances

- If we cancel a test
- If you cancel a test and give us at least ten working days' notice
- If you keep the test appointment but the test doesn't take place or isn't finished, for a reason that isn't your fault or the fault of the vehicle you are using

We will also compensate you for the money you lost because we cancelled your test at short notice (unless it was for bad weather). For example, we will pay

- The cost of hiring a vehicle for the test, including reasonable travelling time to and from the test centre
- Any pay or earnings you lost, after tax and so on (usually for half a day)

We WON'T pay the cost of driving lessons which you arrange linked to a particular test appointment, or extra lessons you decide to take while waiting for a rescheduled test.

How to apply

Please write to the Area Office where you booked your test and send a receipt showing hire car charges, or an employer's letter which shows what earnings you lost. If possible, please use the standard form (available from every driving test centre or booking office) to make your claim.

If you would like more information about our standards of service contact

Customer Services Manager
Driving Standards Agency
Stanley House
Talbot Street
Nottingham NG1 5GU

Tel: 0115 901 2515/6

These arrangements don't affect your legal rights.

DSA Head Office

Stanley House
Talbot Street
Nottingham NG1 5GU

Tel: 0115 901 2500

DSA Area Offices

London and the South-East

DSA
PO Box 289
Newcastle-upon-Tyne
NE99 1WE

Telephone bookings by credit card and other enquiries

Tel: 0171 957 0957
Fax: 0171 468 4550
Recorded message:
0171 468 4530

Midlands and Eastern

DSA
PO Box 287
Newcastle-upon-Tyne
NE99 1WB

Telephone bookings by credit card and other enquiries

Tel: 0121 697 6700
Fax: 0121 697 6750
Recorded message:
0121 697 6730

Wales and Western

DSA
PO Box 286
Newcastle-upon-Tyne
NE99 1WA

Telephone bookings by credit card and other enquiries

Tel: 0122 258 1000
Fax: 0122 258 1050
Recorded message:
0122 258 1030

Northern

DSA
PO Box 280
Newcastle-upon-Tyne
NE99 1FP

Telephone bookings by credit card and other enquiries

Tel: 0191 201 4000
Fax: 0191 201 4010
Recorded message:
0191 201 4100

Scotland

DSA
PO Box 288
Newcastle-upon-Tyne
NE99 1WD

Telephone bookings by credit card and other enquiries

Tel: 0131 529 8580
Fax: 0131 529 8589
Recorded message:
0131 529 8592

Other useful addresses

Approved Driving Instructors' National Joint Council

The Secretary
41 Edinburgh Road
Cambridge CB4 1QR

Tel: 01223 359 079

Department of Transport Mobility Advice and Vehicle Information Service (MAVIS)

DOT
'O' Wing
MacAdam Avenue
Old Wokingham Road
Crowthorne
Berkshire RG45 6XD

Tel: 01344 661 000

Driver and Vehicle Licensing Agency (DVLA)

Customer Enquiry Unit
Swansea SA6 7JL

Tel: 0179 277 2151

Driving Instructors Association

The Secretary
Safety House
Beddington Farm Road
Croydon CR0 4XZ

Tel: 0181 665 5151

The Guild of Experienced Motorists

Station Road
Forest Row
East Sussex RH18 5EN

Tel: 01342 825 676

Institute of Advanced Motorists

Iam House
359 Chiswick High Road
London W4 4HS

Tel: 0181 994 4403

Motor Schools Association of Great Britain Ltd

The General Manager
182A Heaton Moor Road
Stockport
Cheshire SK4 4DU

Tel: 0161 443 1611

National Association of Approved Driving Instructors

90 Ash Lane
Halebarns
Altrincham
Cheshire WA15 8PB

Tel: 0161 980 5907

The Parliamentary Commissioner for Administration (The Ombudsman)

W K Reid CB
Church House
Great Smith Street
London SW1P 3BW

Tel: 0171 276 2003/ 3000

The Royal Society for the Prevention of Accidents (RoSPA)

22 Summers Road
Acocks Green
Birmingham B27 7UT

Tel: 0121 706 8121

DSA THE DRIVING TEST

Printed in the United Kingdom for The Stationery Office Limited
O/No. N0014577, 5/97, C400, 210272, 25038